M000223818

Pieces of a Whole Heart

Pieces of a Whole Heart

Cory Standinger

RESOURCE *Publications* · Eugene, Oregon

PIECES OF A WHOLE HEART

Copyright © 2021 Cory Standinger. All rights reserved. Except for brief quotations in critical publications or reviews, no part of this book may be reproduced in any manner without prior written permission from the publisher. Write: Permissions, Wipf and Stock Publishers, 199 W. 8th Ave., Suite 3, Eugene, OR 97401.

Resource Publications
An Imprint of Wipf and Stock Publishers
199 W. 8th Ave., Suite 3
Eugene, OR 97401

www.wipfandstock.com

PAPERBACK ISBN: 978-1-6667-0631-4
HARDCOVER ISBN: 978-1-6667-0632-1
EBOOK ISBN: 978-1-6667-0633-8

07/22/21

Contents

Broken Pieces

Abuse shattered my heart in pieces,
as if a stone had hit a glass window.
Which had left me puzzled,
how would I put the pieces back together?
My mind predicted bad weather,
I knew once the winds came, it would stir up things.
Picking up the phone, I could hear the rings,
anger started rising when no one answered.
After that, the birds were flying in,
building nests and quickly becoming pests,
they kept building on each other,
till my house was smothered.
Cut my hands from cleaning up their crap.
As the pain increases,
I injected the lies,
being chained to perfection,
brings a connection to protection.
I had no understanding of what was happening,
just that my heart was panicking,
the endless rapid beating,
like waves eroding away the shoreline.
My inner child feeling the pressure, found a haven.
Left out in the cold, harsh world.
All he had left was my coat,
then sailed away in the wooden boat.
While I destroyed my house and moved into the prison.

Anger

Anger can lead to danger.
Sometimes it feels like a stranger,
but others it feels like a familiar friend.
A friendship that does not end,
by sending letters,
that make me feel better,
but only temporary.
It consumes my heart like a wildfire,
a wildfire that refuses to be put out.
People will scream and shout,
because they were burned.
The mind tosses and turns,
eventually it is outpaced by the fire.
The fire will not grow weary or tire,
it will engulf everything till it is dust.
Love rained down over the ashes,
putting the fire back where it belongs.
Out of the ashes a beautiful red rose grew.

Loving Yourself

I have two options,
believe the lie or the truth.
The lie is like wearing a coat,
that I use to cover up.
It brings comfort and warmth,
because the world is a cold place.
I never take the coat off,
people start to define me by the coat,
it becomes a part of me.
I begin to add to my coat,
because the rest of my body becomes cold.
I see other people wearing the appropriate clothing,
I begin to hate myself,
but I keep pressing on because I am warm.
The truth is like a campfire,
which heats me up.
I deny it and make excuses,
then I start taking the coat off.
I feel very cold and hate the feeling,
but the feeling is growing stronger.
I take off everything,
it begins to feel comfortable.
I throw the coat into the fire,
it has brought life to my cold body.
My heart begins to open,
the fire shoots into my heart and closes the door,
once my heart is warm, the rest of the body follows.

The Robe

Caked in dirt,
Saved by the Savior.
Covered in blood,
Reborn as a child.
Cleansed by the living water,
Seen as an adult,
Clothed in righteousness and humility.
Brought up as a warrior,
Chosen by armor.
Treated like a prince,
Crowned by the King.
Ruler over the kingdom,
Cares for the people.

Chains of Containment

Held captive,
in a straitjacket.
Surrounded by walls,
only one way out,
which is always open.
Shouting for help,
does not seem to be working.
I gave into the fear.
Pictures are on the walls,
to remind me of my faults.
The nails drive deeper into me,
I begin wishing for death,
but it never comes.
My heart becomes hard.
Fear floods the room,
it reaches the ceiling,
Where a light bulb is.
The light bulb bursts,
a fire emerges,
burning on top of the fear.
Flickers of light shine through,
I cry out one more time.
The ground shakes,
the walls fall,
the locks are broken,
the nails are pulled out.
I begin to walk towards the light,
not knowing what happened,
having faith, it will not harm me,
hoping it will heal my scars.

My Cup

My cup spilled on me,
so embarrassing.
Shame rushes over,
as people laugh.
Anger wanting out of his cage,
shouting with rage.
Holding my tongue,
not sure why.
Trying to be a better person,
than the people at the party.
But I end up painfully laughing,
trained in high class acting.
I deserved a golden globe,
while I wrap myself in shame's robe.
It is too tight in some areas
and too big in others.
Wishing I stumbled into this prison drunkenly.
Wanted acceptance, so the steps were soberly.

The Cross

Our hearts were closed,
His hands were opened.
Our hearts were selfish,
His hands were selfless.
Our hearts hated,
His hands loved.
Our hearts held on to lies,
His mouth poured out truth.
Our hearts were made clean,
His body was made dirty.
Our hearts were comforted,
His body was beaten.
Our hearts were healed,
His body was broken.
Our name was, "Free them!"
His name was, "Crucify Him!"
Our hearts doubted,
His hands believed.
Our hearts came to life,
His body no longer had life.

Belief

How do I believe in God?
While pain and suffering exist, people prod.
Been through abuse, where was God?
I am constantly doubting
and in anger, constantly shouting,
at God.
Trying to control Him, lightning rod.
Through good deeds, wicked are my ways.
Excuses come and go like the days.
God revealed His power will be shown in pain.
Clinging to that truth only lasts for a while, hope drains.
I need more than that and I fear that is it.

Pursuit of Perfection

I am running this race,
perfection out in front.
Outstretched arms
and falling to my knees.
I ask God, "What am I doing wrong?"
The heavens open,
blood pours out
and covers me.
A voice calls my name.
Not a voice of blame.
But one filled with grace.
"Stop running this race!"
"Come, be still!"
"And be filled with my overflowing love!"
I answer the voice, "I do not have anything to offer!"
It calls out, "You have a heart!"

A New Heart

How do I live with something new?
Cannot hold anything anymore, turning blue.
Do not deserve anything new.
I break everything, it is what I do.
Not sure why God wants to use me,
I am nothing special, sounds more like me.
What does God see in me?
I am covered in dirt and unclean.
Unfit for His presence it seems.
I cannot accept His grace and salvation.
Then God will ask too much of me,
need to earn salvation through works, starvation.
Because I fear what God could ask of me.
Trust is thrown on the big screen,
see the cracks clearly, I scream.
Not sure how to change my trust in fear,
to trust in God.

The Cup of Suffering

The cup poured out,
what we thought was comfort,
but Jesus knew it was suffering.
We began to drown in our sorrows.
Jesus drank from the cup,
till we were standing on solid ground.
The blood of Christ flooded in,
which brought strength to us.
Swallowed by the robe of blood.
Then came the purest form of love,
water rained down.
We began floating to the top.
Drops of blood stayed behind,
they are the safety robes,
which we can hold onto when we slip.
Your cup can either be your destiny
or it can be a destructive device.

Love Responds

What is love?
Why does it captivate?
But how?
Can you grasp love?
Can you understand love?
Do our hearts have what it takes?
Love is not demanding,
but it does depend on a specific person.
A person who is selfless.
Patience is needed,
because they will bleed.
Humility is a must,
because we all came from dust.
Out of love we were created,
this is always debated.
Lies are declared,
Truth has been prepared.
A people divided,
hate was invited.
Spread through the hearts like fire.
Burning the rooted trees,
the fruit was looted.
Love needed a response,
the reply was you before me.
The seed of truth was planted.
Out of the dust grew trees, strong as ever,
rooted in truth and nurtured by living water.
Therefore, love is proof,
purpose is found in community.

The Lion's Voice

A roar in the heavens.
Oh, my heavens!
The lion and the lamb.
Coming down, pure and innocent as a lamb.
But strong and courageous as a lion.
To save the dying.
With arms raised,
I fell to my knees.
The truth grew up through the cracks.
Satan tried to silence me,
with sexual abuse.
But God gave me His voice,
one that roars over the rain.
My identity is not called shame,
I am a child of God.
I step forward in victory.
These dirty, heavy clothes fell off,
then I put on the robes of righteousness.
Crowned with love,
standing firm with armor.
I declare the truth to all,
protector of the people,
responsible for righteousness.

Permission

My child, have no fear.
The perfection that you sought,
the anger that had you in shackles,
the sting of suffering you have been through,
you were silenced by tears of shame,
the walls you built by waves of distrust.
Those cups have been poured out,
cleansed by the living water.
The cross spread out the seeds of truth,
to be planted in tremendous tragedies.
Take off those shabby clothes of shame,
you have been clothed in righteousness and humility.
God gave you His voice,
one that roars over the rain.
Step forward for the crown.
Put on the armor of love,
it will fit perfectly, like a glove.
Because no one can take your place.
Your cup, once filled with your tears,
has now become a light for all.
Shining brightly inside and out.

Lights, Camera, Truth

Truth does not start with me,
it was shown on the cross.
I cannot be the gardener,
roses would confuse me.
Humility is not a close friend,
but pride is my enemy.
Love is not a feeling,
it will always be a decision.
Hate surrounds my heart,
love found the way in.
Sacrifice parted the waters,
even though everyone wants to be a hero.
We want glory to be upon ourselves,
fame brings pressure never seen before.
Burdens will weigh us down,
until we start to break down our walls.
Suffered in silence happens daily,
but it will show through our "diseases."
The cost of our life is priceless,
but we always put on a price tag.
We seek after attention,
but do not want people to see our flaws.
We pursue pleasure,
then wonder what our purpose is.
We want a pain-free life,
but comfort comes with a cost.
We commit suicide to fit in,
but standing out gives us numerous reasons to live.
We hate "real" people,

but want reliable friends.
We want you to be open minded,
but we are closed off to your mindful thoughts.

Happiness

What is happiness?
Why is it valued?
Why do we chase it?
Can we grasp it?
I tend to sabotage my happiness,
thinking on past mistakes, rejections, and failures.
I become engulfed in shame.
What a deadly cycle this is,
around and around I go.
Trying to outrun the next cycle,
only to find I was hit from behind.
Instead of running I dug a grave.
Maybe I thought I was being brave,
masking my identity.
God called me out of the prison of comfort,
by sending His son to die on the cross.
I can either learn to be happy in suffering,
or die chasing something that will not fill me.

Relational Beings

Relationships are like building houses.
The foundation begins with God.
It will take time for the cement to dry and harden.
Once it does, you can start building with it.
Jesus will supply the wood and tools,
He will tell you what the blueprint says,
but He will not show you the whole picture.
You begin building the first floor,
walls are put up to keep you safe.
Then the floor covers the basement,
it protects you from falling into a pit.
Working on the second floor can be delicate.
People may only want to build the first floor with you,
then leave you to build the second floor by yourself.
But you became encapsulated with the planned fantasy,
that you lost sight of what they wanted.
Wasting your time and energy building.
But instead of burning it down,
you leave it up to be a reminder,
for the next person, who comes along.
Your foundation does not change,
but how you build does.

The Casted Heart

A broken heart is like a broken bone.
First the Doctor resets the heart,
then He creates a mold of the heart.
Then constructs a cast for it,
which prevents further damage
and lets the process of healing begin.
He prescribes medicine and instructions,
I felt frustrated with the restrictions.
Comparison begins ravaging my mind,
complaints rise to the surface,
conversations turn toward fits of rage.
Constant pursuit leads to a changed perspective,
slowly over time acceptance comes around.
Despair leads towards hope,
complaints lead to compliments.
The cast is removed completely,
the new heart will take time to adapt.
The heart's desires will ring true.
The promises will push through,
allowing for deep rooted growth.

A New Light

I pressed on because
the blood-stained cross caught my muddy soul,
the vision of trust captured my tear-filled eyes,
the broken body bought my undeserved freedom,
the innocent blood covered my sinful desires,
the soothing voice swooned my stone-like heart,
the boulder-like burdens became the blueprints for blessings,
the walls of pride were humbled by truth's persistent cracks,
the path less traveled intersected my unguided steps,
the jingling keys lead my shackled feet to leap with joy.

Deep Waters

Anger deeply rooted,
shame ensnares.
A seed of perfectionism planted,
which is overgrown through my boundless fence.
The gutsy flesh is fighting back,
like a tidal wave crashing over me.
A battle, I am quickly losing,
because the doubts are rising.
My demons are drowning me in these condemning waters.
My suffering has suffocated my hope,
my despair has torn down my trust.
The surrounding walls are holding the water inside,
the stone-like walls are shaping my heart.
My strength has fallen short,
my body became lifeless.

Outcast

The devil is swinging my sins,
in front of me, hypnotic.
I am psychotic.
Seduced into a trance.
Drooling from the mouth, I pranced.
Slapped around, abused.
Dazed and confused.
Chained up, bruised.
Fed lies, birthed loathing.
Feelings buried, dying.
Alone, bypassed.
Impaired and trespassed.
Seeking relief.
Reeking of a false belief.
Fortified the castle walls.
Pressure from the King reigning His calls.
Crown in hand, refuse surrender.
Stuck in a closet as a pretender.
Uncover the masks I wear.
Shame began to tear.
Control was disrupted.
A little boy interrupted.
Casted out of comfort.

Prison of Comfort

The art of self-sabotage,
the self-permission towards rage.
The chains seem so faintly,
but the scent is felt strongly.
This cage has been crushed by the Vine,
but conditioned to stay within the lines.
Walking around this prison till exhaustion,
mentally asking, shouting, "Where is the salvation?!?"
These tears of shame provided the shovel,
to which these emotions were enclosed in gravel.
Invitations were sent out for their funeral,
but all people did was walk on their burial.
Family and friends have come to visitation,
collected pages of maps to joy and hope.
But mentally unavailable to climb the mountainous slope.
The guards want to play "Red Rover, Red Rover."
Been listening to the same lies over and over.
Those words hypnotized my voice to silence,
that psychotic grin comes from the internal violence.
Someone wake me up, this is not a dream,
tied to this bed of control, tearing at the seam.

Composure

I was a clown,
I hid my pain behind this smile.
I used to go the extra mile,
to make you happy.
Now the demons will not let go,
they know I am no average joe.
I finally escaped this cage.
I must be all the rage,
because they are hunting me down.
Time for a change,
Anyone have loose change?
Nope? I will just put my time in this ride.
Where is my Guide?
I will just turn around and walk in that direction.
I must have lost Him when I was in the house of mirrors,
because I thought I was not capable of making errors.
The food and game stands would hold me back,
then I would not have any slack.
Asking people if they had seen my guide.
Some say yes and others replied,
"You are the guide of your life."
But I recall seeing Him before,
back at the house of mirrors with a knife.
Time to slice up these demons that walk through the door.
My thinking is usually unorthodox,
I am coming at you like a jack-in-a-box.
This may be a surprise to some of you,
but I am trying to scare these demons.
They can only wind me up for so long,

before my emotion's breakthrough.
The demons must have brought the lemons,
because something sweet was coming all along.

Afraid

The voice has broken through.
What will I do?
I cannot handle this burden.
It began in Eden.
I am standing on the verge of breakthrough.
When will I let go?
And fall into the ocean of grace.
I feel like a disgrace,
for running this race.
But I do not know my place.
These bottled feelings are like mace,
but instead of keeping people at bay,
I ran away.
Pride had a place on my porch,
I never acknowledged it was overgrown.
I trimmed it up to be like a beautiful flower,
it always needed a shower.
I finally planted it into the ground,
I woke up to find myself in a jungle.
Nasty surprises at every corner,
trying to uproot it, poisoned me.
I needed help, but how do I ask for it?
I lost myself in this jungle,
screamed till I could not hear anymore.
The darkness blinded me.
I started to climb a tree,
never had a strong on hold it.
The fetal position became the only option.
I surrendered to hopelessness,
then my heart adjusted to the darkness.

Honesty

Standing in the darkness,
once again homeless.
Walking towards the light,
Should my hope be as high as a kite?
The jitters in my stomach,
come from being around the public.
Can I become uncomfortable,
by eating at the wrong table?
Address the messiness,
my heart adjusted to the blindness.
Addicted to the control.
The constant patrol,
over everything that steps on my porch.
Bring the torch,
burning this jungle down.
I am no longer a clown,
I want you to be proud.
That should not be said out loud.
It is not really my type,
this fruit is unripe.
Smoking the peace pipe,
inhaling the incense.
Do not give your two cents.
Trying to overcome these emotions,
built an overpass.
Once again bypassed.
Learning about barriers,
then they became the carriers.
Which provided protection,
then revealed a reflection
of the afflicted.

Safe Place

Wanting freedom from this prison,
but I find safety in my room.
Alone and in control,
where I can bloom.
I need a constant resting place,
the abuse wears me down.
I lay in this bed of comfort,
my mind blows around the doubts.
I struggle to turn it off,
the shivers push me to the edge of an attack.
Layers of lies wrap me in warmth.
Shame drove me mad,
Will I ever be glad?
It held perfection above me,
wanting me to struggle for it.
These layers of lies held me back,
I completed suicide internally.
Passion and dreams floating in my head.
Afraid of what happened before,
I left the dreams at the curb,
just in time for trash pickup, superb.

Pieces of a Whole Heart

Time for honesty.
Standing up, I looked around this dim-lit prison.
To see I was in a straitjacket.
I thought I created a safe place.
But I drank from the cup of suffering.
Everything was dying from the internal violence.
The deep waters started to rise,
the light bulb burst causing a fire to break out.
I could not keep my composure.
No longer a clown,
whose emotions were a jack-in-the-box.
But I had self-sabotaged my happiness while I was hypnotized.
And afraid of what happened before,
I became an outcast,
on a journey to pursue perfection.
But being dazed and confused led me to a jungle.
Since I been here before, I had the blueprints.
I was finally seeing in a new light.
The jungle was set ablaze with my anger.
My treasure from searching was the truth.
I built a kingdom around the cross in which I wore a robe.
Then the armor of love covered me perfectly.
I gave permission to my heart to roar over the ashes.
Then out of the ashes, a beautiful red rose grew.

Weathered

Obsessing over self-glory,
falling into the great abyss,
no quiet bliss.
The cold winds remind of bitterness,
whispering lies of hate.
Holding onto the weight,
do not take the bait,
this should not be on the plate.
The heart of stone is a work of art,
being carried on a cart.
To be thrown in the ocean.
Setting into motion,
the lack of emotion.
The demotion to a love potion.
Sipping on it,
became the bridle and bit.
Playing the Romeo and Juliet skit
and memorizing the script.
Perfection only brought depression.
This is not only a confession,
but a truth digestion.
The jitters in my stomach are back,
but it is not time to cutback.
Just reeling in the flashbacks.
Putting the stones together,
to build a foundation for the weather.

The Numbness

Everything to gain,
from numbing the pain.
Overdosing on comfort,
took too many chill pills.
No one around to split the bill,
no time to chill,
relaxing is out for the kill.
Laughing it off,
with a scoff.
Walking around the abyss,
notice the emptiness.
Blinded by the darkness.
The depravity is the gravity,
weighing on me with insanity.
The answer is simple and out in front.
I need to let go of the face paint,
which tainted my pocket.
And throw away this heavy locket.
Which only has a picture of a clown.
When will I be wearing a crown?
Reminding myself of who I am.
Time for a second medical exam,
constantly wanting growth.
My heart seems to be under oath,
new condemnations rising.
Advising to see the disguising.
Like a fish realizing, it was mistaken about a lure.
Hooked and dragged on a detour.
Which has led me to a café,
where I am part of a buffet.

Feeling bloated from eating only lies,
reading the bottle for the capsize.
Realizing the support of an evil enterprise,
uncovered the nasty surprise.
A heart transplant was needed.

Self-Hatred

The darkness is back,
paint the walls black.
Dim the lights,
it is too bright.
Eyes straining,
it is raining.
Dreaming of greatness,
my heart feeling the numbness.
Crucifying myself,
anger nailed down the feelings.
Walking across on the bypass,
outcast to the outside.
People do not understand,
I hate myself, not them.
People brought up feelings, resurrection.
But isolation provided protection.
Every step loosens the nails,
it is time to bail.
Unless you want to pay my bail?
Maybe it will be better if you leave,
that is what I believe.
I honestly want to share everything,
but you do not see the rejection sting.
Thinking on the condemnation and shame,
wondering who else needs the share of blame.
Because I do not want to remain the same.
Perfection does not find itself,
but it sits on a shelf.
Like a golden calf.
My heart was torn in half,

just like it was choreographed.
Stuck in a trance,
as I continue to prance.
No longer listening to my conscience,
But am I even conscious?

All of Me

Struggling to give my all,
as if I was given no call.
Distracted by other things,
like the consequence will not sting.
A choice is to be made,
just not under the shade.
With no other options left,
saying yes is like theft.
But I am only working hard when it matters,
then my heart shatters.
Like biting into a sandwich,
to find it was filled with sand.
Which tastes gritty.
Maybe I will stop asking for pity,
strength is what I need.
Tired from pulling the weeds
and changing into the appropriate clothing.
The old self is moaning,
while the new growth is showing.
Little by little,
quick to belittle.
Comparison is a projection of neglect,
but the timing is perfect.
Comes down to acceptance
and repentance.
Talking like I am in attendance,
but stuck in adolescence.
Just as a flower takes time to bloom,
what happens next is all consuming.

Beauty from Ashes

From the ashes arose a rose.
Wearing no clothes.
Such a beauty under the nose.
Caution should be used.
Thorns protect the abused.
Just a warning to the confused.
Encased for all to see.
Waiting on the care and attention that it needs.
Such integrity and innocence.
Standing out with a bold, bright red.
As if it was a reminder of the bloodshed.

Social Anxiety

Staying up late thinking,
eyes blinking.
Courage shrinking,
false belief reeking.
Cover up with a sweet scent of self-hatred.
Holding hands with my insecurities,
keeping that relationship sacred.
Judging the impurities.
I let people pass by,
because I am the shy guy.
No cheating, staying loyal.
Perfection flirting, as my insecurities boil.
Trying to be social, while anxiety is calling.
How can she be ignored when no one else is calling?
Or she must be pushing them away.
What should I tell myself?
That it is my fault they are gone.
Why bring blame into this?
He would just bring up shame
and how she has a deep-seated kiss.
Deep secrets and deep pain are her game.
Anxiety called me but shame did the talking,
she told me I will never be good enough.
Brushed it off as I continued walking.
When will someone else stay and not leave?
Then the truth would be easier to believe.
Is it time to shed this straitjacket?
Won't the dislocation of my heart be unbearable?
Sharing the pain is irreplaceable.
Maybe I need to run away from myself,

as I sit on this shelf.
People must not like the scent of self-hatred,
blowing out the fire in my heart like it's a wick.
Now the darkness is less favored.
Why is the analogy a candlestick?
If not for a candle, what would be my identity?

Lonely

Walking on this healing journey alone,
just staying up late at home.
While in agony,
finding my apathy.
Smiling with a calmness,
inside is a growing desperation.
Changing the thirst to numbness.
Fixated on the frustration,
the sadder I become.
Only given the crumbs.
People must see me as chewing gum,
as they twiddle their thumbs.
The taste must be gone,
spit out and stepped on.
All I want is to belong.
But living withdrawn,
shades drawn.
Closing off everything.
Am I lost or confused?
I do not know anymore.
Found a safe place at least,
in quiet, thoughts released.
Out comes the beast,
where the demons feast.
True self deceased,
with the same walls of distrust.
Which held the water of grace.
As the walls fall,
grace spreads to all.
Acceptance was a struggle,

but holding onto it is a juggle.
Loneliness is a creep, who will always stalk.
Peeping through the windows, waiting to strike.
But he does not knock.
He scares you with a presence that is birdlike.
Who is to say he will not follow you,
when you hang out with people,
or even at the steeple.
Overcoming is a steep hill.
Because phoning a friend leads to shame answering,
"Why bother someone with this burden?"
Everything is interconnected like a spiderweb.
Following one strand leads to an overwhelming feeling.
A feeling of fear before the spider draws near,
or is it as the spider draws near, fear begins rising?

Inner Child

Raised in pain,
while hate became the rain.
Conditioned in the barren lands.
People pleasing became the strands.
Putting their needs first, excessively.
Their happiness becomes an idol, oppressively.
The driving force,
as a dark horse.
Self-aware of who I am not,
the spider's strand tying the knot.
Suffocating, losing myself.
Should have stayed in the boat,
the bitter cold winds are causing a sore throat.
Feeling under the weather, where is my coat?
Drowning became an escape,
because the mind is a videotape.
Rewind over and over, studying every detail,
revealing what's underneath the veil.
In the barren lands toxic gases inhaled,
then in community control exhaled.
Healing pulling me closer to the waterfall.
Doubts swimming in my head, cell wall.
"But do I want the healing?"
Shame is questioning.
Because healing can cause more pain, drained.
Even though I reached the prison's ceiling.
No way but up, uncomfortable.
Sitting at the Devil's table.
Like a knight at the round table.
Telling this false king, freedom is the desire.

He draws his sword and I start to perspire.
Feeling trapped in a corner in the room with no walls,
reminding myself to think of the waterfalls.
A photogenic mind which has not lost the maps.
As more and more walls collapse,
it seems like no time has elapsed.

Till Death

As walls collapse,
because of the book of maps.
Light shines through the gaps,
hope overlaps.
Safe place invaded,
fresh air inhaled.
Found a rose on a dusty path.
Regaining self, releasing the wrath.
The past becoming a skeleton,
love turns my heart into gelatin.
Down the path is the wooden boat.
While the fire burns this wool coat.
Rowing down the river, away from this island.
Working towards the highland.
Mountains to valleys, breathtaking.
Decision-making is painstaking,
but it leads to the peacemaking.
Buried my old self properly,
into jars of pottery.
Not to hide but to remember myself,
which sit on the shelf.
Locked away in my heart,
not to ever depart.
But to realize the abstract art.
I fell apart, to be set apart.
For a greater purpose.
The heart is a complex body part,
Who can understand it?

The Wooden Boat

Carried my inner child away,
kept him safe day after day.
While the storms arose,
causing waves to have highs and lows.
It had the proper clothes.
I sent him away.
Because I wanted to protect him.
But really, I needed to grow up.
Or so I thought.
Found a blind spot.
Stuck in adolescence.
Self-hatred's essence.
Like the candle was dipped in a protective coating.
While lit, the candle starts smoking.
Filling the lungs, choking.
Could not breathe, knocked the candle over.
Burned down the house, nothing leftover.
Made it out alive, but at what cost?
Knowing my inner child is somewhere, feeling lost.

Rescued

Building an altar,
on the once standing prison, alter.
Such a sight,
a picture of the whole heart in the light.
Coming out of the darkness,
seeing through the blindness.
The fire coming from the heavens,
instead of from within, which deafens.
Baggage left to be the bricks,
no longer carrying sticks,
but only a crucifix.
Some would say that is a heavier burden,
but I can lay down this burden.
To create a bridge for all the pits,
Are you ready for the battle of wits?
The devil will use scripture against you,
turning your heart black and blue.
Shame could cause a stomach flu,
but you have had your beef stew.
God rescued me from self-destruction,
now I can function.
No more time to slack,
the bills were beginning to stack.
Indebted by God's measuring level,
Jesus made it level.
Just need faith that is the size of a pebble,
to move mountains, tremble.

If Only

My mind sometimes replays the abuse,
like a broken record, the heart blues.
The lyrics reminding what could have happened,
if the abuse did not happen and
if only I had the courage to stand up.
Drank from the self-blame cup.
Found comfort in food,
changing my mood.
A mindset of guilt and pleasure,
like finding a secret treasure.
X marks the spot to a tombstone.
Lead astray to loneliness.
Thinking I had all the pieces.
Happiness decreases,
hatred increases.
I watch others have self-discipline,
while I stand in the buffet line.
Soul left unsatisfied,
the abyss became wide.
Inside I died, food enthroned.
But outside I lied, God dethroned.
Such a white-washed tomb,
as I sat in the washroom.

Silence

Inside the washroom,
lays a picture of freedom.
Such a powerful image.
Silent as He stood accused.
As we looked upon Him, confused.
Even though for our amusement He was abused.
The bruises and scars were not refused.
Not only for a glimpse of freedom, but for an eternal love.
Which we were void of.
Never understanding what our void desired.
Trying to cleanse our imperfections,
in a washer and dryer.
While our bodies became dirty again.
Transformation starts in the brain,
then the rest of the body comes next.
Just like taking a shower, specs.
On the backside of the picture is a subtext,
which has left us perplexed.
Fighting each other as if freedom were never given.
But really, we hate that we have been forgiven.
It is too complex for our simple minds.
But love has set us free, as our lives unwind.
Which points back to one who showed love first.

Unbelief

The darkest part,
of my heart.
Do not look,
it is a closed book.
Misplaced trust,
begins to rust.
My heart becomes toxic,
so exotic.
Still wanting to look strong,
I paint over it.
People do not see the wrongs,
unwilling to admit,
or unsure how to.
Anger buried; bitterness grew.
Picking off the fruit,
adding the secret ingredient, dilute.
Drunk off the wine, such foolishness,
wondering why this joy is eluding us.

Fear

Scarcely loved,
deeply buried.
From the past,
seems to last.
Those heavy chains,
suffocating the veins.
Moving into survival,
needing revival.
Pushing everyone away with their arrival,
thinking everyone is the same,
they are given blame.
Anger and anxiety shown,
an aching in the bones.
Weighed down by stones,
sinking deep in these dark waters.

Realization

The spirit stirred,
self-awareness unblurred.
Realizing the God-sized hole.
Like looking at the keyhole,
to see no key is present.
Using other keys as supplement,
as pride smirks.
Like clockwork.
Wishing to rewind the clock,
to prevent the stumbling block.
But instead, read the manual.
To manually fix the mechanical.
Build a relationship with the mechanic.
Because the manual does not cover everything, panicked.
Or it touches more on some topics than others.
Less on buffers
and more on the engine.
Here come Satan's henchmen.
Such an obsession,
to steal and destroy the joy.
Using women from playboy.
But I am not the flesh's delivery boy anymore.
Ran to the garage door.
Locked the car away,
before they cause decay.

Trust

After the trauma,
I lost all trust.
Built up walls,
to ignore the name calls.
Just want peace and quiet,
the voices are not being silent.
Thinking people were the problem,
but brokenness is the problem.
What is needed is healing,
my heart is bleeding.
Trust has been misplaced before,
listening to pastors and people, who stand at the door.
Handing out blow pops,
something is left out, jaw drops.
The middle,
selling tickets to a game, dribble.
Yet, my mind was tickled.
Entertained as a goat,
thinking I was the "GOAT."
Days passed, I became angry with God,
I felt entitled for His blessing, odd.
God challenged back with silence,
being patient with my misplaced reliance.

Traction

Found traction in Christ,
no longer slipping on ice.
Spring has sprung, melting away the ice.
The rocks bring a bumpy ride,
but I am driving an all-terrain vehicle.
The top of the mountain looks unreachable.
But that is too critical.
Because where I stand is a miracle.
Seeking grace for my harshness,
especially in times of darkness.
Sitting in the presence of God, listening.
Then learning,
about the Father's heart.
Then speaking the desires of my heart.
This relationship is like fine art.
Peace and rest are found,
where perfect love is bound.

Joy

Seems unobtainable,
but being surrounded by God, unrestrainable.
A posture of internal worship.
Leading to a glorifying relationship.
Through connection of the Vine.
Awakening the spirit of the blind.
The key to fear's bind,
a daily constraint.
Like a child with finger paint,
free of worries, guarded by the Father's presence.
Such a pleasance.
An undeserved grace,
for this mishandled race.
Love sprouts from that seed,
which bled for the creed.
Baggage fell off.
Feeling lighter, lift off,
to a different heart space.
A higher level of thinking, a slower pace.
One filled with peace,
where everything existing, ceases.

Love

Perfect love, a heavy weight.
Almost crushing, like an open flood gate.
With multiple tries, still a failure.
Even with a feeling's tailor.
Need a grace unrelenting,
ever so repenting.
Listening is the backbone,
then patience and compassion are shown.
Speaking comes next,
so, peace and rest are the effects.
Control the tongue like it's a sword,
as it's being removed from the heart of stone, broadsword.
Water breaks apart the stone,
leaving behind a firestone.
The spirit igniting a flame,
purifying the stabs of blame.
Internal wounds inflamed.
The roses' thorns holding together the pieces, vulnerable.
Pricked on the slightest touch, intolerable.
Love was pricked but did not leave,
How was I to believe?

The Voices

Doubters speaking,
peace weakening.
Angrily shouting in my head.
While laying on my bed,
curling up.
Knowing I am not good enough,
shame filling my cup.
Other voices in my mind,
being so kind.
Challenging those false things.
Sounds like self-help,
which does not help.
Another one is whispering
and leaves my ego withering.
It is heard above the noise,
bringing many joys.
Straining to listen.
Stuck in this sin,
lusting and sexual fantasies.
Apologizing, then back to old behavior.
Manipulating the Savior.
Abusing grace,
laughing at the race.
Thinking I am a winner,
but I am only a beginner.
Feeling pressures on being holy.
So, I walk lowly.
Now who is holey?

Grace

Living in disbelief,
washed with awe and grief.
Cause God is a perfect being,
not that He is agreeing or unseeing of my sin.
But it is covered with innocence.
Providing a sweet fragrance,
awakening my sleeping spirit.
Drawing closer to God, inspirit.
Lacking understanding to why.
Thinking I was a good guy,
saying to that mentality, goodbye.
Humbled by the actions of God.
All glory to God,
for taking us off the throne.
By using the stone.
Setting into motion the keystone,
which is above the fireplace.
Forming the workplace.

The Goodness

God's goodness was shown,
in the garden, His throne.
Once deceived by the snake,
the heart's break.
Left thinking God is not good
and He was withholding, misunderstood.
Madly in love with other gods.
Especially at calling myself a god.
Shame drove me to protect myself.
While God sits on my shelf.
Next to things of unimportance.
But given significance.
A fool's gold,
with a stronghold.
Such a strong hold,
on a broken chest.
God not given the best.
But the grace He has for my worst,
leads to thoughts reversed.
Looking at the cross, bloodstains.
Reminds of God's goodness amidst the worldly pains.

The Tree

As the blinds open.
Peer into the windows.
To see shadows.
Of the once standing fears.
My eyes are filled with tears.
Because on the wall are memories,
which have created documentaries.
Wisdom was gained,
to tame the untamed.
Now as I walk underwater,
it separates, by my heavenly Father.
Much has been said,
to the heart's threads.
But the truth brought it together.
Such a tether.
Jesus gave his last breath,
so we could see through the darkness of death.
As the curtain was ripped from top to bottom,
it brought a beautiful autumn.
From inside I finally see,
the thriving fruit tree.

Panic Attack

Hidden internal screams,
the body shakes.
Skin crawling,
blood boiling.
Shame piled up,
darkness in my cup.
I hate myself,
over my sin.
Just want relief,
from false beliefs.
Hidden pain,
covered by rain.
Stuck in the grave,
not sure how to be brave.
Buried alive,
the flesh is in overdrive.
Causing panic,
pushing the manic.
Just want to please God,
thinking perfection is the answer, odd.

Left Behind

Scars left on my heart,
what an art.
From people's choices
and voices.
Mistakes, which left me triggered.
Bitterness left behind, undelivered.
Walking down dark tunnels,
vision funnels
on the small passages.
While God slowly shows the big picture,
who is the victor if I become sicker?
Not what was pictured.
God's glory will still be shown,
over time, I have grown.
Darkness may surround.
Sight is drowned,
fear's playground.
But waiting, is faith's greyhound.

Invalid

It stems from seventh grade,
when a girl called me an "it."
Cut deep, degrade.
Still dealing with it.
Constantly lusting,
longing,
for a woman to validate me.
Out of answers,
so many questions.
My mind wrapped around the lie, tightly.
Like a child's hand around a parent's finger, securely.
Such a relatable picture.
Not what is pictured.
Trusting the lie is like stranger danger,
but trusting them anyway.
Lost the way.
God, I need help.
Asking strangers for help.
But a friend points back to Christ.
The snow prevents slipping on the ice.

Who I Am

At first, the abuser and abused.
The oppressor and oppressed.
A disgraceful sinner.
A passive winner.
Bitter and hard-hearted.
Sharp-tongued and strong-willed.
Always grasping at revenge.
A rusty door hinge.
Idolizing everything in sight.
Yet blinded by sight.
Then Jesus restored my sight.
Now I am a child of God.
Created by and for God.
His prodigal son,
whom He loves.
Forgiven,
and has unmerited favor freely given.
Not from what I have done,
but because of who He is.

It is Finished

For when comparison comes up
and when shame piles up.
Spiraling into cycles of defeat,
struggling with disbelief.
Leading to a tornado-like destruction,
losing my house again, happiness abduction.
Thinking on change, hoping in wrong things,
moving my focus onto the true King.
He provides faith for my unbelief,
which allows me to walk on deep waters.
A hope for my hopelessness,
through His plans and purposes.
Creating beauty from ashes,
while my kingdom crashes.

Reputation

Gaining a certain rep.
People pleasing swept,
under the rug.
Graves dug.
Mask of death found,
People only see good, not the hellbound.
Worried about true self,
being seen by others, clear shelves.
A boxed-up life.
Left in attic, dusty life.
No one has seen the attic,
it would cause panic, static.
Such a fear of rejection.
Assumption's projection,
using old photos.
No new photos,
to use against the fear.
Besides the one found in the bathroom.
Where I can escape the safe room
and remove the mask.
To allow myself to clean the mirror's glass.

Hope

Discoverer,
not living under a rock.
But standing on the rock.
To withstand the weather.
Not acting like a feather.
Hope rises,
like a lighthouse, holding different prizes.
A King who suffered a death then resurrected.
Relating to the suffering, physically.
Beginning to see the resurrection, mentally.
Forming the emotion of love,
feeling like a glove.
Providing the protection,
sought after from fear, strategies detection.

Stress

Keeps filing up,
the glass cup.
Once it overflows,
made it to the cove.
Starts the panic,
the edge of the manic.
Acting out, like a child.
Having an episode, seen as vile.
Alone, while on the mountainside.
Body shaking but not cold,
bones aching but not old.
Tired but cannot sleep.
After time, back to normal.
Forgetting the abnormal.
But not without weeping.
Crying out for God's keeping.
Wondering if He sees, silence.
Or hears my violence.
Am I forgiven?
When the uncontrollable is given.

Love's Emotion

Scared to love someone,
to feel love from someone.
Always suppressed emotions,
worried about showing the explosions.
A volcano's eruption,
causes destruction.
Just want to hold back,
rejection is not giving up any slack.
Childish, I know.
The heart receives the low blow.
But self needs preserving.
Being vulnerable left me hurting.
Trusting left me devastated.
Seems understated.
I killed love,
with gloves.
But caught red-handed.
Branded as a traitor,
needed a savior.
Who wants to save a murderer?
Brought in as guilty,
Jury found me guilty.
Deserved death,
yet, love showed grace.
By coming back from the grave, He won the race.

Rejection

The greatest fear.
The reason for letters beginning with dear.
Writing to God, showing my darkest fears.
Giving Him my cares and anxieties,
my thoughts and abilities.
So many pages and words,
of the same words.
Not sure where the fear came from.
Struggling with it.
Called an "it."
Intentionally but mistakenly,
like I was meant to be someone else.
Wearing a mask to be someone else,
rejected and neglected by the world.
Learning to take off the masks,
because I am accepted by God.

Dear Abuser

Writing to you, from anger.
From what happened in high school.
Sexually abused, treated like a tool.
Of pleasure.
Like my body was a secret treasure.
For you.
Leaving my heart black and blue.
Shame arose.
From wearing no clothes.
Frozen in fear.
Because rejection was near.
Bitterness grew up,
through my cup.
Poisoning the water supply.
Carried for five years, everything alive dies.
Walked the path of death.
Thinking perfection and self-hatred brought wealth.
Time given to this mental prison.
But He has risen.
Freedom bells ringing.
Doorbell ringing.
Answered, while staring at the floor.
Grace stood at the door.
He entered,
and I was restored.
Dear abuser,
you are forgiven.

Was That You?

When I asked God to reveal Himself,
memories of the abuse kept popping up.
God showed me He was near,
while my body lay bare.
God provided strength to me,
by stirring the voice in me.
He was there, just not in the way I thought.
Cried tears of grief and relief.
God is still working on my heart, belief.
Emotions are walking out of the grave,
love rains down, helping them to be brave.
What a beauty seeing them firmly planted,
alive and chanting,
"Glory to God!"

The Journey

Finding my voice,
in the desert, choice.
People will come across me,
asking, "Who I am supposed to be?"
Thinking on my response,
knowing their wants.
They seek a well which does not run dry.
As I speak of hope, some will cry,
while others will not.
Because they feel too far in shame's knot.
Gently pointing them towards the well, a seed planted.
Instead of letting the seed of rejection be planted.
People will scream for attention, deserted.
Pride and shame perverted,
the voice of men.
We will not stand tall in the lion's den.
God's word can be heard over our shallow words,
protected from demons with His words.
Because Jesus bore our sin and shame on the cross.
The devil took us across,
the street to see pride.
While Jesus went looking for our sheep's hide.

A Child Again

Dear God,
how can you love me?
As fear lingers over me.
Can you change me?
Into whom I am supposed to be.
To have a child-like faith.
From broken and confused,
to healed and fused.
Not a ruse,
but the fuse.
Truth replanted.
False identity removed.
Innocence restored.
Falling into the Father's arms.
Finding comfort, no harms.
The feeling of safety washes over,
like a blanket cover.
Trusting again, a childhood vent.
Which blows out a familiar scent.
One that seemed lost.
Because the abuse reminded me of the high cost.

Abandoned

Emotionally aching.
Chasing relief, body waking.
Left alone by family and friends,
in times of need, trust ends.
Where was God, doubters speaking.
Heavy burden on my being.
Cannot change the past,
it was not meant to last.
But it did, truth hurts.
Not trying to be curt.
No one is listening though,
Maybe God is, stuck in dough.

Breathe

Walking into church,
anxiety waiting on her perch.
Rather stay in the safe room,
because I cannot hide impending doom.
Feeling judged, overwhelmed.
Going home, self-hatred.
Laying on my bed, crying.
Shame washes over, dying.
Running to masturbation,
thinking it is a savior, spiritual castration.
Keep me afloat false god.
Sensitive to sin, isn't that odd?
Out of answers and ideas,
of what to do next.
Cause guessing has led me nowhere.
Can someone care?
Is that too much to ask.
But that might not help to empty the flask.
Longing for acceptance and to belong,
while I feel worthless, doubts gong.

Finish Line

Finishing the race,
may never come in this lifetime, not a disgrace.
But victories will be experienced.
Breakthroughs lead to hope.
Hope leans on trust, walking the slope.
Difficult to trust God, I built stone walls.
Even though Christ rolled the stone away, to me He calls.
Could not handle the discomfort.
Effort was given for my kingdom, a pillow fort.
Do not want to let go of my hard work.
Disillusioned, the pride smirks.
Crawling towards the finish, perfection in first.
Focused on perfection, instead of Christ.
Created a reality where I am superman.
Feeding myself according to my plan.
Called it a diet,
but drinking like a pilot.
Crash landing,
so much for planning.
Humility created a new vision,
learning the truth comes with a decision.

Help

A cry of desperation,
towards God, losing respiration.
End of myself,
when will you step in for me?
Cause I see no way to go.
I am falling below,
these dark waters.
Hard to see you in pain, waiter.
Identity was stolen,
but I thought things were golden.
Even in the present, I did the hard work.
The debt must still be there, from the hurt.
How is the debt paid?
Because the self has made,
the decision.
Unbelief, such precision.
I tried to be precise,
but it was worthless, roots need sliced.

Hurt

Holding back the waves of anger,
before the danger.
Overtime, anger erodes the shoreline,
unspoken words rumbling around in my mind.
Acting like God was blind,
thinking His silence was unkind.
Pain, with no understanding of why.
Blame the unseen, telling myself I am a good guy.
The heart hardens towards love,
while He suffered for His beloved.
The feelings are valid but not reliable,
left frustrated but wrestling with God, dependable.

Refuge

Feeling feelings,
makes me angry, chilling.
Telling myself to stop,
like I am a cop.
Finding shelter,
in the Savior's suffering.
Suffering can lead to a numbed heart.
Suppressing feelings, a poison dart.
Unraveling the heart brought intense feelings.
Ones too much to handle, always kneeling.
But sometimes pride can seep in,
wanting God to leave, a shark fin.
Mistaken about who God is
and the love He has for his kids.
The cycle continues,
until the truth fights the insecurities.

Soft Heart

Healing led to peeling,
off the layers, tough skinning.
Sensitive to people's words.
A new heart hurts.
Choose to follow old cycles
or take a new tricycle.
Accept the alive, beating heart.
Instead of adding tough skin, a dart.
Learn to forgive quickly, compassion.
Hurt people hurt people, grace's ration.
Leave the past, grieve.
But the pain will be the gas, believe.

Thank You, God

An underused phrase,
but still one of worship and praise.
Thank you, God, for our multiple chances,
because of your love and grace.
For showing us forgiveness,
time after time, such a kindness.
Justice, when we seek you,
while revenge leaves our faces blue.
Going through the process of death,
to give us a spiritual breath.
For truth, to tear down lies,
because it is hard to say goodbyes.
For listening to our cries,
when we try and fail, and hope dies.
A hope for the future,
by your plans and purposes, nurture.
For your ways and thoughts being higher,
because self-destruction is dire.

The Whole Heart

Piece by piece.
Being rebuilt, brokenness ceases.
Creating an altar for God the Highest.
Filled with worship and praise, saying goodbyes.
Accepting the daily stress,
through carrying this cross, distress.
Dear abuser, did you find what you were searching for?
While I always feel left behind, closing doors.
Causing panic attacks, breathe.
Rejection drove me to protect my reputation, grieve.
Searching for who I am, the journey.
Finding the source of hope, it is finished.
Helping me love again, found traction in Christ.
Because of His refuge, thank you, God.
Sincerely, your servant.

Made in the USA
Middletown, DE
23 October 2021

50870737R00050